The
A·T·H·L·E·T·E·
Formula

A 7-Step Guide for Coaching Athletes Toward Peak Performance

by Robert Levine, Psy. D

AUTHOR'S NOTE

Three things inspired The ATHLETE Formula. 1) I am a psychologist and love the study of human behavior. 2) I am a lifelong sports fan; I can die happy because the Chicago Cubs finally won the World Series. 3) My son, R.J., was not athletically gifted but started to play soccer.

My wife and I wanted R.J. to play sports for the physical activity, the social interaction, and because if it were up to him, he would sit and play video games all day. When R.J. was eight years old, he started playing in a soccer league. Unfortunately, R.J. did not have a very good coach and he became upset and frustrated. When he was nine years old, my wife and I had to twist his arm to join soccer again but with a different coach. He was hesitant but reluctantly agreed. I watched his first practice. All the other players were more skilled than him. R.J. became dejected and walked around the field with his hands in his pockets.

Practice finally ended, and R.J. strolled off the field with his head down. He lifted his head up. With a sad face and in a voice that just makes a parent want to cry, he said, "Dad, I'm not any good. All the other kids are better than me. They run faster and they kick the ball away from me. I can never get the ball. I'm just not any good." I thought about encouraging him by saying that he is a good player, but I did not think that R.J. was delusional. Anybody with two eyes could see he was not a good soccer player.

So what did I say to R.J.? Some may say this is sacrilegious and something you should not say to your child, but I said, "You know what, R.J.? You're right! You're not very good! You might even be the worst player on the team!" I figured honesty was the best policy. I then explained to him that everybody can contribute to the team. I described how he could do small but important things to help his team. I remarked that he could do things like slowing down a player on the other team just enough until the rest of his team could make it down the field to help him, or he could dive for loose balls.

I then explained to R.J. that soccer was never my sport. However, I was always a big basketball fan. I told him that there was once a basketball player who was certainly not as good as players like Lebron James or Kobe Bryant; his name was Shane Battier. Shane did a lot of little things to help his team, like playing good defense and diving for loose balls. Because of Shane's willingness to do the little things, his teams usually made the playoffs and even won a championship a couple of times. I then proclaimed to R.J., "You're the Shane Battier of your team!"

R.J. looked up at me and realized a new perspective on his soccer life. He no longer felt inferior to other players on his team. R.J. knew his role and embraced it. He did not feel substandard and less of a player but that his team needed him.

At R.J.'s next practice, he looked like a whole different kid. He had confidence and seemed to feel great about his new role on the team. After the first game, a coach commented about how well R.J. played on defense. One of the parents on his team even nicknamed him "the minister of defense." Over the years, R.J. has continued to improve at soccer; he has started to play offense and has begun to contribute to his team even more. His soccer coach helped him develop his physical skills while I focused on some of the mental and emotional aspects of the game that helped him bounce back after initially feeling dejected.

The concepts in The ATHLETE Formula are designed for athletes at nearly all levels of performance who have at least a basic level of understanding and skill in their sport. I understand the physical abilities of a professional athlete are different than a Little League player. However, the basic mental and emotional premise remains the same, regardless of skill level. Humans are generally more alike than they are different. For instance, R.J., like all athletes at all skill levels, cannot perform well and improve if his mental and emotional states are not in a good place. From this idea, The ATHLETE Formula was born.

Soon after I came up with the concept of The ATHLETE Formula, an interesting thing happened. The Olympic games began in 2021 (it was postponed for a year due to the COVID-19 pandemic). World-class gymnast Simone Biles took herself out of several events after she began suffering from emotional difficulties during an event. Some people called her a "hero" for bringing light on a national stage to mental health and the emotional difficulties she was suffering. Some people demonized her for not being there for her team; what kind of backlash would NFL great Tom Brady experience if he did not show up to a playoff game because he was feeling too depressed? All are valid arguments. Regardless, my perspective is that it was clear that she and her team focused on her physical capabilities but not enough on her mental and emotional state. The ATHLETE Formula is designed to help you coach and train your players to work through such difficulties.

I would like to thank my wife Becky and my sons R.J. and Ryan. Becky has been with me through a lot of thick and thin in my life, and I'll always be thankful for her. She has told me for years that I should write content, but I never knew what. My sons mean everything to me, and I have used The ATHLETE Formula principles with them. I especially want to thank R.J. for ultimately improving in soccer after his initial struggles. It certainly validates the effectiveness of The ATHLETE Formula.

Later on, another inspiration for The ATHLETE Formula materialized. I came across an episode of Malcolm Gladwell's podcast Revisionist History called "A Good Circle" (Season 8, Episode 11). In this episode, the sportswriter and author Mitch Albom explained a lesson he learned that was discussed in his book *Tuesdays with Morrie* and said, "Taking makes me feel like I'm dying. Giving makes me feel like I'm living." So I want to give a gift to others and create a legacy so I can feel like "I'm living."

TABLE OF CONTENTS

INTRODUCTION

So you decided to be a coach. Congratulations on joining this amazing fraternity! There are many reasons people make this decision. One of the main reasons is that people want to see the impact they make on others. The beauty of coaching in sports is that there are many definable metrics. If, over time, a baseball player increases his batting average by fifty points, that's a sign of definable improvement. If a basketball player increases his free-throw shooting by 10%, that is also a sign of improvement.

I'm Dr. Robert Levine, and I've been a clinical psychologist for over twenty years. I have worked with government officials, the military, law enforcement, and business professionals to help them create the mental edge they need to succeed. What I realized was that the issues facing these various professionals were similar to those who participate in sports. All of them viewed success as being defined by results, but they often lacked the necessary process. Rarely is anybody such a prodigy that they can will their way to greatness. To achieve success, people need systems, methods, and the ability to bounce back following periodic setbacks.

How do we help your athletes perform better? Yes, I know: just keep practicing until they're gold medal machines. That would be nice, but your players are not machines, and they never will be. Machines can do the same thing repeatedly until they break down. Humans can break down much quicker without proper maintenance. Machines often come with instruction manuals. While I am not brave enough to say that I've discovered the athlete's instruction manual, I will say that I have constructed a guide to help you improve your athlete's performance and help him bounce back after a setback. My goal is to help you and your athletes become the best you both can be.

The ATHLETE Formula program provides a simple, user-friendly, actionable methodology to help coaches help their athletes improve their performance in a given area or bounce back from setbacks that can include slumps, disappointments, and injuries that can be physical and/or emotional. The ATHLETE Formula is a seven-step program rooted in true and established psychological principles tailored to help athletes achieve their maximum potential.

*For simplicity, I have used male pronouns (i.e., he, him). However, let me be clear that this is **NOT** a gender-specific program. The concepts in the program are universally applicable to anyone who is trying to improve his or her performance. While every person has strengths and weaknesses, The ATHLETE Formula program is there to help coaches help their athletes discover areas of improvement and incorporate psychological principles to better hone such skills. These principles run universally throughout humans, regardless of gender or other demographics. The ATHLETE Formula applies to anyone trying to coach others to improve their mental edge.*

The ATHLETE Formula is a seven-step program that helps coaches and trainers address the mental and emotional aspects of sports within their athletes. What does this mean? In brief:

I'm taking concepts in my field that I've learned from a lot of smart people with a bunch of degrees who have done tons of research on psychology over the years. This material was in books and journals that you will probably never read. So, I'm taking these concepts, simplifying them, and giving you the playbook to effectively engage your athletes. Makes more sense now? I thought so! However, in the unlikely event you do want to read more about these and other psychological concepts, I have included a resource for you.[1]

As you read through The ATHLETE Formula, *keep in mind that* sports is a microcosm of life. Even the best loses more than they win; remember, the best baseball players typically get out seven out of ten times. Whether a person makes a long career out of sports or eventually realizes he can no longer excel on the playing field, the lessons of The ATHLETE Formula can be applied to most walks of life. The ATHLETE Formula is a guide to help humans manage inevitable failure and develop resiliency.

---

1   Wenzel, A. (March 23, 2021). Handbook of Cognitive Behavioral Therapy. American Psychological Association (APA).

THE THREE-LEGGED STOOL

What I have discovered through research and my own experience is that top performance and a person's ability to bounce back are based on a three-legged stool. The three-legged stool involves components that are a) physical, b) emotional, and c) mental.

If an athlete is missing part of that stool, he will be compromised. This is the case at most levels of athletics, from early on to the most advanced. Someone may be able to "fake it" for a little while, which might result in some early wins. However, missing parts of the stool will ultimately result in a person's demise. This demise often takes the shape of frustration, burnout, and/or not achieving the long-term success that is desired.

The three-legged stool of athletic performance are the physical, emotional, and mental components. Why are these components so important? Imagine a stool that is designed to have three legs. Unfortunately, one of the legs is missing or is not attached properly. What happens then? When you sit on the stool, you are likely to tip over. At a minimum, the stool is uneven and wobbly; it is difficult to sit on and uncomfortable. In an extreme case, could result in you falling and getting hurt.

The three-legged stool of athletic performance is very similar to a real stool. If one of the three legs is not functioning properly, the athlete is likely uncomfortable and, in extreme circumstances, could result in an injury.

PHYSICAL

PHYSICAL: For the purposes of The ATHLETE Formula, this is the perceived ability to engage in a task. There are no apparent tangible reasons why an athlete cannot at least eventually perform an athletic task or perform an athletic task better. For this leg of the stool to be intact, an athlete, for instance, is not suffering from a severe arm injury that is preventing him from effectively shooting a basketball. The Physical leg of the stool is considered intact if the athlete "could" perform the athletic task but is unable to because he was not properly trained OR is engaging in diminished performance for non-injurious reasons, such as being in a slump.

PHYSICAL DISCUSSION: You are coaching players. All your athletes have some level of talent and have probably been playing for some time. This is not their first rodeo. Maybe you're coaching at the middle school or high school, you are the coach of a major college athletic program, or you are coaching professionals. Regardless, you are coaching athletes with some level of talent. Maybe you can help your pitcher throw a better curveball, challenge your football team to run a different scheme, or suggest that your golfer hit a ball with a different club. Regardless, you have little doubt that your players can perform most tasks given to them with proper coaching and training.

HOW DOES THE *ATHLETE FORMULA* HELP WITH THE PHYSICAL LEG OF THE STOOL? Ultimately, the Physical leg of the stool is what coaches and athletes care about. The athlete needs to hit the ball better, shoot better, run faster, and/or throw better. That is the end goal. The athlete "might" simply be doing something that impairs his success. His hands are not gripping the club properly, his legs are too far apart in the batter's box, or his arms are not high enough when he is shooting. If adjustments like that are all it takes to get your athlete to perform at the desired level, then congratulations! Your ATHLETE formula journey is done! Now go play ball! Unfortunately, oftentimes the difficulty with the athlete runs much deeper than minor physical modifications. So for all the rest of you, your ATHLETE formula journey now continues.

EMOTIONAL

EMOTIONAL: Let's discuss the emotional component. The ATHLETE Formula plays a role in this regard. Do you have players who seem to be passionate about competing? Does competition excite them? Do your athletes like to compete even if they are overmatched? Do you have athletes who are excited about competing even if there is no chance at a scholarship or some other pot of gold? If you answered "yes" to all these, then your player likely has the necessary passion for the Emotional Leg of the stool to be a good athlete. One of my favorite examples of passion is by Hall of Fame baseball player Rickey Henderson.

Passion: Hall of Famer Rickey Henderson

Rickey played nearly twenty-five years in the major leagues for several different teams. He won almost every individual award imaginable, won the World Series twice, and earned millions of dollars over his career; he is, by all accounts, financially secure. However, how did Rickey end his career? Did he go on a Major League farewell tour? No, the last time Rickey played baseball as a professional was with the San Diego Surf Dawgs in an independent baseball league. Rickey simply loved to play baseball and did not seem to care what capacity he was playing in.

However, do you have an athlete who seems like the last thing he wants to do is go to practice? Do you have a physically gifted athlete who lacks the desire to compete? Maybe his dad was primed to be the town's local sports hero until he blew out his knee. So, your athlete was "forced" to live out Dad's dreams, but it has turned into a nightmare for him. Does he seem uninterested or that your criticism doesn't affect him? Is he unwilling to do the "little extras" to improve? If this is going on with one of your athletes, then no amount of yelling, screaming, or threatening will get him to improve. He might be able to get by on a certain amount of innate ability, but his potential will be thwarted by a limitation on this leg of the stool.

Sometimes, a player might be going through difficulties in his life that he is having trouble blocking out. Often, someone hears about the great athlete who views the playing field as his sanctuary where he can block out troubles in his life. Unfortunately, that is not the case for everyone. Sometimes, things like family problems are too overwhelming for an athlete to concentrate on his athletic tasks. Once he learns how to deal with this problem emotionally, his passion may return. These are often temporary situations where you, as the coach, can help him through. Maybe you can be a good listener or provide resources to him. Another thing you might be able to do is ease up on his practice regimen temporarily. It could be the task he's being asked to do is something he has not mastered yet. Maybe most of the rest of the players have mastered a skill that he has not. Do not generalize! That just makes things worse.

Provide him with the extra training he needs to get up to where he needs to be. You might be surprised at how giving a player a little extra time on the front end can pay major dividends on the back end. When someone is struggling, it is important to ask him to limit his scope by focusing on fewer or easier tasks.

As a coach, you are used to seeing an athlete suffer an injury, such as a broken foot or a sprained ankle. Often, after extensive rehabilitation, the athlete can return to form; sometimes, he never does. This is similar to an athlete and his emotions and whether he can bounce back after something difficult happens. He might return to form, but there is also the possibility that he never does if there was never truly any passion. Other times, there is a lack of passion because the athlete is not playing for the "love of the game" but is playing for "secondary gain." Secondary gain could mean that he is playing for a large contract, a scholarship, or parental approval. This can last for a while. It might even be able to last long enough to achieve the immediate goal that the athlete is looking for, such as a scholarship. Unfortunately, eventually, the athlete's true colors will be seen. At some point, he will not give extra effort. He will not pay attention to the details. Your athlete will ultimately be burned out. At this point, it will be difficult to have his passion and performance return to where they were before.

Burnout

There are different types of burnout, such as emotional, mental, and physical. This section will focus on the emotional aspects of burnout, which are very much intertwined with one another.

Burnout is difficult to overcome and rehabilitate. This can commonly occur in athletes who have played for any length of time, such as since childhood. You think you are a good coach because you are supporting your players to maximize their potential, and you were always taught that "practice makes perfect." At the level you are coaching, you have athletes who have some level of athletic proficiency. However, suddenly your athlete wants to quit because he is burned out. He struggles with some of the basic athletic tasks. A little break or counseling with a psychologist might help. Unfortunately, this is frequently a long, difficult road to recovery. That is why taking care of the emotional side of the athlete is equally as important as the physical side. What makes this more frustrating is that the emotional side is harder to observe. The athlete does not put a cast around his emotions the way a person puts a cast around a broken arm. There is no X-ray where he can see a fracture and watch the progression of recovery over time. Nonetheless, burnout requires similar levels of care.

There are things to keep in mind to prevent burnout. More physical and/or emotional stress is only better up to a certain point. Once an athlete is at the level of burnout, more physical and emotional stress further diminishes performance. See the curve below, which is known as the Yerkes-Dodson Law.[2] Optimal performance occurs in the middle area, where there is the proper balance between physical and/or emotional stress and performance. This arises when reducing physical stress is important, such as when your athlete suffers an injury. In these situations, less physical stress over a short period while they rehabilitate and recover will ultimately result in an increase in performance over some time. The same idea holds true when dealing with conditions discussed in the Yerkes-Dodson Law, including burnout.

---

2   The Yerkes-Dodson law is a model of the relationship between stress and task performance. It proposes that you reach your peak level of performance with an intermediate level of stress or arousal. Too much or too little arousal results in a less effective performance. This is also known as the Inverted-U model of arousal.

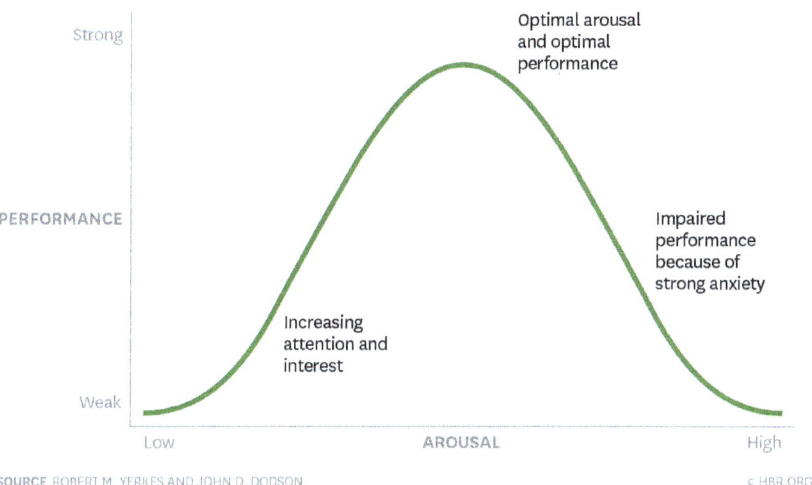

Effort

There are some exceptions to this, like when an increase in effort is needed. When a quarterback is running the two-minute drill, he needs to engage in an increased effort and focus over a condensed period. This level of effort can achieve quick, high-impact results, but this level of focus is not sustainable over a long period of time. Sometimes, situations arise when a person needs to sprint. A sprint, like a two-minute drill, is designed for a short period of ultra-high impact. This level of effort is not sustainable over the marathon of a season.

Finding that middle ground for the particular athlete is the key. This could mean having the sport you coach him in but also finding a healthy diversion for him that gives him joy to help him recharge. Too much time spent on one thing can lead to the premature ending of a person's career. Burnout does not look like an injury like a torn Achilles tendon; however, it functions similarly. Overusing any part of your body, physically and emotionally, can be damaging. Both physical and emotional damage can have similar effects on a player's career where he struggles to function properly.

Do Less, Not More: The (Tennis) Ball is in Your Court

Tennis legends Serena Williams, Venus Williams, and Andre Agassi are three of the greatest players ever in their sport. Their accomplishments are virtually unparalleled. These three athletes have put a tremendous amount of effort into becoming great. Surprisingly, at the early stages of their careers, they each were criticized for not being fully committed to tennis. They were pursuing various other interests. What each of these greats discovered was that burnout is a real thing. While many other tennis greats, such as Bjorn Borg, achieved early success but ultimately faded out well before they were thirty years old, their true greatness only lasted about ten years due to their unwavering focus on tennis. Serena, Venus, and Andre were able to prolong their great play for at least twenty years or more!! Overemphasis on one aspect can eventually produce mental and emotional fatigue. All these great tennis players put a LOT of work into tennis. However, some realize that clichés like "giving it your all" or "giving 110%" were not a recipe for sustained career longevity. Mental and emotional fatigue are just as real as physical fatigue.

Emotions are hard to measure and quantify. Sometimes, they get a bad reputation. We are often told not to listen to our emotions. However, it is a vital leg of the stool that helps explain the ebbs and flows of the athlete's successes and failures. This leads to another leg of the stool that can also be hard to measure, which is the "Mental" leg.

MENTAL

MENTAL: Coaches often spend extensive time on the physical side but neglect the mental side. Once many of the fundamentals are understood, most games are mental. How do you prepare your players for competition? How do you prepare them to win? Maybe more importantly, how do you prepare them to lose? Is it right to prepare to lose? I thought that we were supposed to think positively. If we think positively, then we cannot lose! Right?? Or maybe there is another side to positive thinking, where a person prepares to fail and learns how to bounce back after a loss?

This is where The ATHLETE Formula can help. The processes in this program are designed to help athletes achieve the mental edge to get from below average to average, from average to good, and from good to great. It is designed to help coaches help athletes who are trying to bounce back from a slump or who may need some redirection. The ATHLETE Formula is designed to bring athletes' confidence back up when they're down and work through situational anxiety. This program is also extremely effective in getting athletes through some of their toughest challenges, and it demonstrates how coaches can help their athletes manage through the "thrill of victory and the agony of defeat."

While people often think about the physical and, sometimes, the emotional part of sports, what separates the haves from the have-nots is the mental part of sports. If you master the mental part of sports, you can play chess while your opponents are simply playing checkers. You can coach athletes to be a step ahead of much of the competition. Most importantly, developing a mental edge helps prolong the victories and minimizes the effects of losses.

One can argue that much of sports and life is learning how to bounce back from failure and adversity. The best hitters in Major League Baseball get out seven out of ten times. The top scorers in the National Hockey League do not convert on nearly 90% of their shots. NBA legend Kobe Bryant holds the dubious record for the most missed shots in NBA history. Nobody ever wants to lose or not succeed, but learning how to pick yourself up after a loss is how the great ones achieve success. It is an athlete's resilience that keeps him or her going, evolving, and learning, which is what makes someone successful in current and new endeavors. Do not focus on the positives or the negatives, but help your athletes focus on thinking critically. Help your athletes strive but bake in that failure is a *major* part of the game that will always be part of it. The beauty of sports is that nobody ever achieves success 100% of the time; in baseball, one might say that nobody bats a thousand. Thankfully, it only takes small, incremental improvements to cause big changes. I once told someone, "If a baseball player gets out eight out of ten times, he's likely going to have to seek out a new career. If he just gets out seven out of ten times, he's going to be an all-star." Averaging one more hit every ten times at bat does not seem like much, but it is ultimately a life-altering accomplishment.

When coaching for an effective mentality, consider some of these rules of thumb:

- Have your athletes spend at least 60% of their time on the trusting mentality and no more than 40% of the time on the training mentality.[3]

- Focus on the target and less on mechanics.

- Quality of practice is more important than quantity.

- Trying harder is not trying better.

- Slim margins and consistency add up to a gap between you and others over time.

- Focus on progress over perfection.

- Being the best doesn't mean you always win, but it means that you win more than others.

- Your biggest opponent is yourself. Your observable opponent makes you better.

- Don't look at the scoreboard.

- Making a good play that didn't work isn't a failure.

- Focus on the basics.

- Even if you are running against others, run your own race.

- Goals are for people who care about winning once. Systems are for people who care about winning repeatedly.

---

3   This essentially means to focus more efforts on the mental and emotional legs of the stool and less on the physical leg. Too often, there is disproportional focus on the physical leg, and the mental and emotional portions are marginalized.

16

HOW DOES THE ATHLETE FORMULA WORK?

The ATHLETE Formula is a seven-step program that helps coaches and trainers address the mental and emotional aspects of sports in their athletes and recover following adversity.

This program is designed to help those who coach and train competitive athletes to improve their performance edge in their given athletic pursuits. These lessons are universal for almost any kind of performance improvement. Whether you are coaching intermediate athletes or professionals, these lessons are designed to help beyond the fundamentals.

What follows on the next page are relatable examples of situations that are commonly encountered at various skill levels. Think about how you can use these principles to work with your athletes.

***ATHLETE** formula* **Steps**	**Brief Description**
<u>A</u>spiration	The general goal for the athlete, like running faster.
<u>T</u>roubleshooting	Focus on the specific problem and the definable solution, such as increasing speed in the 40-yard dash by 0.5 seconds.
<u>H</u>ow We Think	This is the self-talk, such as when an athlete says to himself, "I'll never be able to get that fast."
<u>L</u>iving with Emotions	These are the feelings that the athlete is experiencing, such as being depressed because he can't run as fast as he wants to.
<u>E</u>xude Confidence	The athlete's belief that he can improve by becoming aware of the thoughts and feelings he has about himself.
<u>T</u>actics	Start practicing the physical skills needed to achieve improvement, such as initially having the athlete try to run 0.1 seconds faster. Then gradually increase this speed over time.
<u>E</u>valuate Your Legacy	Passing your knowledge and wisdom onto others. Show and/or tell other coaches and athletes what you found successful to help them succeed.

Once upon a time, focusing on a player's mental needs or his "feelings" was often code for him being *soft*; that's a term nobody wants to be called. This program is designed to help your athletes deal with inevitable adversity and not "choke" or "shrink" under pressure. The goal is to help you coach your athletes so they can rise to the occasion in sports or any other chosen endeavors.

One important thing to remember about The ATHLETE Formula is that it is a process. It is not a quick solution done immediately before a playoff game. The ATHLETE Formula needs to be done over time. If you are looking for a quick solution, do your best with the concepts in this book, but reading it quickly without understanding each of the steps and concepts is not the optimum use of the program and won't lead to miracles. This is a multi-step system or process to work through with your athletes. Throughout your journey with your athletes, there will be inevitable periods of success, failure, and mediocrity. My goal for you is that you will help your athletes cope with each of these periods constructively and predictably. It's my intent that The ATHLETE Formula is as straightforward and user-friendly as possible.

CHAPTER 3

ASPIRATION

The first step in The ATHLETE Formula is the Aspiration step, where the athlete's overall goals are defined.

The definition of "aspiration" is a will to succeed or a cherished desire. In Latin, "aspiration" means inhalation or breathing. When we aspire to do something, it means we breathe life into it.

STEP 1: ASPIRATION

What do you want from your athlete? What do you want your athlete to develop? Maybe your athlete suffered a setback and is trying to recover or "bounce back" to return to form. What are some goals that you would like your athletes to achieve by the end of the season?

During Step 1, Aspiration, think in more general terms, such as wanting the athlete to have more stamina or training him to hit better or field better. Maybe your athlete suffered an injury. The physical injury has recovered, but now he is struggling to perform for fear of re-injury. This is the aspirational step, so it is okay to dream. Dreams are what keep us going. This is going to be the big picture or your athlete's "Why."

Remember when you were seven years old and people asked you what you wanted to be when you grew up? You might have said you wanted to be a doctor because you wanted to help people who got sick, or you wanted to be a pitcher to hear the roar of the crowd after you struck somebody out to end the game. When you answered this question, you did not think about the years of medical school or practicing the wind-up for hours on end. You thought about the end result. This is the idea of beginning with the end in mind.

Work with your athlete on developing his aspiration. It is often important to figure out why this might be so important to him. This "why" is what will keep him motivated during difficult times. As you move through the program, you will see the "why" turn into a method for "how" the aspiration will be achieved.

The important thing about aspiration is that everything should be under an athlete's control. An aspiration to win MVP, become the starting shortstop, or land a scholarship to the player's dream school is out of his control or just puts him back to where he was before the slump. All these scenarios have outside forces affecting them. This could simply mean other athletes are better than him or there are outside forces at play, such as the athletic director telling the coach to put in a particular player because his father is an influential booster. I am not saying that these things are right, but they happen, and a person must learn how to deal with them. The ATHLETE Formula is not designed to help an athlete in a vacuum where he has complete control over his destiny. The reality is we do not have complete control over outside influences. The purpose of The ATHLETE Formula is to help develop resilience so the athlete has the mental and emotional bandwidth to cope with real-life changes in sports.

ASPIRATION: Super Bowl Champion and Wide Receiver Torrey Smith

At one point in his football career, Torrey Smith was not a starter but committed himself to being a good practice player. Torrey was once named "Practice Squad Player of the Year." He kept on improving and was willing to be adaptable. Over time, his opportunity arrived when he was promoted from the practice squad player to starting wide receiver on the Baltimore Ravens and helped them win the Super Bowl. Torrey did not know when or if he would get promoted to the team. He could not even be certain if his opportunity would occur on the Ravens or if he would have an opportunity to compete for the Super Bowl. Torrey focused intensely on what he could control. He did not want to be on the practice squad, but becoming the best possible practice squad player was all that was in his control at that point. Eventually, his preparation as a practice squad player met an opportunity. Torrey ended up having a good NFL career. Can I guarantee that you will be successful like Torrey Smith? No. However, if you focus on what you can control, as Torrey did, you are putting yourself in the best possible scenario to succeed.

METAPHOR: *When a farmer plants seeds, he cannot guarantee the crops will grow. It could be unseasonably hot or cold, or an unknown virus could kill all his crops. However, the farmer's job is to plant the seeds, water the soil, and care for his crops appropriately to create the best opportunity for a good harvest. Your job as a coach is to help harvest your athletes.*

As a coach, you might have different desires for your athlete than what he has. Talk to your athlete. Find out what his aspirations are. If your plans are grossly out of line with the athlete's plans, then the likelihood of success is going to be very small. This will lead to negative consequences such as animosity, frustration, resentment, and ultimately, poor performance. Work on trying to bring each of your aspirations greater in line with each other. Just like any relationship, two people may need to compromise to focus on a singular, strongly defined aspiration.

Example of How to Have an "Aspirational" Conversation

ATHLETE: Hey, coach! I want to be the starting shortstop on the team this year.

COACH: OK. What do you think you need to do in order to get there?

ATHLETE: Well. I don't know. I think I got better last year, and I think that job should now be mine. Maybe all I need to do is get on base a little bit more.

COACH: Well, it doesn't quite work that way. I've got a bunch of guys on this team who think they can be starters. I also think you have more that you need to work on other than just getting on base more.

ATHLETE: What do I need to do?

COACH: You need to do better at fielding ground balls. Also, you need to get on base a lot more often through hits and walks.

ATHLETE: OK. How can I do that?

COACH: Definitely practice more, and I'll also get one of the assistants to work with you on your plate discipline and fielding. Also, I have a smaller depth chart over at third base. This will get you more opportunities to get on the field and work on those skills. Why don't you try playing third base? There's less competition at that position this year. You can get more playing time and work on your fielding and hitting without the pressure and competition of playing shortstop.

ATHLETE: But Coach! I've been playing shortstop since Little League!

COACH: I get that. I know you want to play shortstop, but to get there, I'm going to advise that you play third base so you have more opportunities to hone some of those skills that apply to third base and shortstop. It'll also be great for me to know that I have a player who can play multiple positions.

ATHLETE: OK, I see where you are going with this. I'll do this if you think it can get me to my goal of playing shortstop.

The above example is the type of conversation an athlete and a coach might have. This example shows that the aspiration is to get more playing time through improved skills. However, there are some outside forces and a lot of competition for shortstop positions that are preventing that goal from being realized. These outside forces are real and cannot be overlooked. Therefore, seek out what is available given the circumstances. Also as a coach, keep in mind that athletes are often competitive and stubborn. In this example, the athlete really wants to play shortstop, but the coach recommends he play third base. Oftentimes, athletes are trained to overcome adversity through sheer force and will. Unfortunately, that does not always work, and accepting harsh realities is a more productive path to success. The conversation in the above example might, in reality, be more prolonged and adversarial.

26

TROUBLESHOOTING

The second step in The ATHLETE Formula is the Troubleshooting step. The purpose of this step is to more specifically define and better assess the problem.

The definition of the word "troubleshoot" is to solve a problem by tracking down its sources. It came from the word "troubleshooter," which has origins dating back to the early 1900s when telephone and telegraph repair workers were sent in to do their jobs.

STEP 2: TROUBLESHOOTING

What does the coach think the athlete needs to improve upon? Does the athlete struggle in certain situations or with a particular task? Does the athlete have a desire to be better at these tasks or situations? Does he want to get better at something? Or is the athlete content with his level of performance? Is there something that the athlete performs well during practice, but in the heat of the game, seems to struggle with? Is he trying to bounce back after a physical or emotional setback?

In the Aspiration step, we look at higher-level goals; in the Troubleshooting step, we dive into the specifics. Like in the previous step, it is important to ensure the coach and athlete are working together for a common goal and the athlete is committed to skill improvement or bouncing back from a difficult period. Dale Carnegie wrote in the classic book *How to Win Friends and Influence People* (Simon and Schuster, 1936) that "a man convinced against his will is of the same opinion still." What I am essentially saying is do not push your athlete too much if he is reluctant. Yes, I know, you read a book or watched on YouTube about a Type A, know-it-all "authoritarian leader"[4] who used force to carve a subordinate into a high-performing creature; you want to incorporate a similar philosophy into training your athletes. Or you get a rise out of watching your favorite coach in a documentary expressing aggressive levels of anger that galvanize the team and take them over the line for victory. Those make great stories, don't they? I will not go into a literature review about the problems with this type of "leadership" and "coaching." However, if you want to look at such material, I have included a link.[5] This "authoritarian leadership" method has a high likelihood of causing unwanted and unintended consequences on the athlete, the athlete's performance, and the athlete's relationship with his coach. The bottom line is if the athlete is not looking to improve at this point, do not force it.

---

4   *Authoritarian leadership* is defined as a "leader's behavior that asserts absolute authority and control over subordinates and [that] demands unquestionable obedience from subordinates." Cheng, B. S., Chou, L. F., Wu, T. Y., Huang, M. P., & Farh, J. L. (2004). Paternalistic Leadership and Subordinate Responses: Establishing a Leadership Model in Chinese Organizations. *Asian Journal of Social Psychology*, 7 (1), 89–117.

5   Pizzolitto, E., Verna, I., & Venditti, M. (April 4, 2022). Authoritarian Leadership Styles and Performance: A Systematic Literature Review and Research Agenda. *Management Review Quarterly*, *73* (2), 841–871. https://doi.org/10.1007/s11301-022-00263-y.

Sometimes, improvement comes more organically or from encouragement from others. Keep in mind that using The ATHLETE Formula is a process that usually takes time. How much time? It all depends on the athlete. Just remember that if you are looking to resolve a performance problem the night before a playoff game, it is best to keep this to yourself at this point and simply tell your athlete to get a good night's sleep.

So, it has been agreed between the coach and the athlete that there is a skill that we want to improve upon or reacquire after suffering a setback. Let's get to goal setting. (See Goal Setting 101 in the Appendix as a quick guide to construct your plan.) Try to be specific about what you want to improve. Some types of specificity might be harder to measure than others. For instance, shooting a free throw is the same process and procedure every time. A person can see how often a shot is made and there is no interference; similarly, running speed is completely contingent upon an athlete's skill and ability. Fielding ground balls or shooting basketballs during the flow of a game has a lot of different variables that you cannot control, such as the trajectory of the ball and the proximity of the defender. Nonetheless, decide what skill you want to focus on. Do not overwhelm the athlete by pointing out a multitude of deficiencies. Focus on one skill to work on improving, and do not worry about anything else for the time being. A game like baseball requires several different skills (hitting, fielding, running, etc.) to be successful. Sometimes, the improvement of one skill will bring about confidence that results in the athlete being able and willing to take on new skills.

There might be other situations where one skill is made up of two separate components. For example, say you have a shortstop who needs to improve on his ability to field ground balls and throw to first base. Fielding ground balls is a skill. Throwing the ball to first base is another skill. The combination of fielding a ground ball and throwing the ball to first base in a seamless set of motions is another kind of skill.

TROUBLESHOOTING: Jason Kidd Can't Shoot!

Jason Kidd is one of the greatest point guards to ever play in the NBA. He was a magician with the ball, a ten-time NBA all-star, an All-NBA defensive player, an NBA champion, and a gold medalist. Since high school, great things had been predicted for Jason. However, there was a glaring weakness to his game that was noted on his pre-draft scouting report. One of the most fundamental aspects of playing basketball is the ability to shoot, and according to the scouting report, "he's not a good shooter." Jason knew that if he wanted to have a long and productive NBA career, he would have to develop his shooting ability. He defined his problem as wanting to improve his three-point shot. When Jason was with the New Jersey Nets in the middle of his career, he worked with the shooting coach, Bob Thate, on ways to improve his shot.[6] Becoming a viable shooter would be an asset to his team and help prolong his career. He had to unlearn everything he had been doing his entire life. Jason learned that he had to do things like getting a better extension on his shooting arm and not turning his body when shooting. He engaged in the extensive practice and repetitions of this new and improved shooting technique. Ultimately, this method worked. At the time of this writing, Jason Kidd has made the fifteenth most three-point shots in NBA history! He began his NBA career making under 28% of his three-point shots but finished his career making three-point shots almost 43% of the time!! Not too bad for someone who is supposedly "not a good shooter."

---

6   Kidd targets a weakness and gives Mavericks a better shot. (2010, April 17). *The Dallas Morning News.*

> KEY STRATEGY: If you are trying to decide which skill to work on, I will typically recommend that you start working on the skill that seems to be the easiest for the athlete. Then, gradually progress to more difficult skills. There are two major reasons for this: 1) If an athlete cannot accomplish an easy task, how can you expect him to do a harder task? 2) Accomplishing easy tasks helps build confidence and momentum to take on more challenging tasks. Remember this for all areas of your life. Did anybody ever ask you to write a term paper at five years old and learn the ABCs in college? I do not think so!

A question that sometimes comes up when deciding on what to focus on is this: should we focus on things that your athlete is already good at but could improve upon? Or should we focus on improving his weaknesses? My response is that it depends. As an example, say you are coaching a basketball player who is the shortest member on your team. It probably does not make sense to work on his rebounding techniques. Developing this skill will be of little benefit to him and the team. Time is better spent developing things like his passing and defensive skills. He might have average skills or perhaps he experienced a setback that affected these areas, but it would be in his and the team's best interest to improve or work on bouncing back in these skill areas. However, say you are a baseball coach and are coaching a player who is a very good hitter but is a major defensive liability. This liability is so significant that it affects your willingness to put him in the field. In this case, it would be in everyone's best interest to improve some of his weaknesses to help increase his playing time. As illustrated in the sidebar about Jason Kidd, Jason focused on his shooting because he knew that this would be a great asset to his team. He also realized that as he got older and wanted to continue playing, being a viable three-point shooter would allow him to continue to be a productive NBA player. As a point guard who is 6'4", which is relatively short for NBA standards, helping Jason Kidd become a better shot blocker, which typically requires more height, would likely be of little benefit to him or his team.

Here is another important component as you work on coaching your athlete. Focus on the athlete's current and improved performance. **DO NOT EVER** compare that athlete's performance with another athlete. The other athletes have nothing to do with each other, and making these comparisons only results in frustration and contempt; I do not care if your starting shortstop is the worst fielder in the league and you cannot understand why he is not as good as the others. Find your athlete's ability and work to improve from there.

> REMINDER: Find what you want to work on with your athlete and make that your mission. Focus on his small improvements to not overwhelm him. Do not focus on perfection but on these small improvements. Decide what you want to work on with the athlete. Concentrate on some aspect of hitting, fielding, throwing, kicking, running, shooting, etc., and stick to that until noticeable and sufficient improvement is acquired over time.

What are noticeable and sufficient improvements? It is hard to quantify and often depends on the skill. Just remember that perfection is not a plan; it is a fantasy. Small improvements can result in a large impact. The best major league baseball hitters get out seven out of ten times (.300 batting average) and become all-stars. A hitter who gets out eight out of ten times (.200 batting average) is likely going to have to think about pursuing another career. Therefore, all he needs to do is make a small improvement by getting one more hit every ten times at bat. This small improvement can completely change the career trajectory of an athlete. Small improvements can result in monumental impacts.

Example of How to Have a "Problem" Conversation

ATHLETE: Coach, I don't think I have a prayer of being a good shortstop.

COACH: Why not? Put in some more time with your fielding and I think you can be really solid.

ATHLETE: But I look at Bobby on the Tigers and he is unbelievable! Nothing gets by him! He looks like he could play in the major leagues and win a Gold Glove.

COACH: Bobby is really good. I think he was getting trained from an early age.

ATHLETE: I'll never be that good!

COACH: That's possible, but don't worry about Bobby! You just focus on where you are. You are running your own race. Paying attention to how great Bobby is of no benefit to you!

ATHLETE: OK, Coach.

COACH: Let's focus on trying to improve your skill of getting in front of the ball quicker after the batter hits the ball. Once we get that down, we can work on how to get more accurate throws to first base.

ATHLETE: That's a good idea, Coach.

COACH: We'll start that tomorrow.

When the athlete starts to feel frustrated and overwhelmed, it is fine to pause for some time and resume at a later point (we'll discuss "pauses" later). Feeling frustrated and overwhelmed often leads to quitting, and we do not want that to happen; do not employ your authoritarian leadership method of coaching. The authoritarian leadership method will likely result in eventual quitting sooner or later. This is all part of the *MENTAL* and *EMOTIONAL* legs of the stool. All too often, coaches default to the idea that success occurs when one tries to push an athlete harder *PHYSICALLY*. Success happens when an athlete is pushed a little bit past his comfort zone ability. That usually means temporarily easing up or employing a new strategy.

CHAPTER 5

HOW WE THINK

The third step in The ATHLETE Formula is the "How We Think" step, which helps the coach to better understand what the athlete is thinking about.

The definition of the word "think" is to have an idea, belief, or thought about something. It originates from the Middle English word "thinken," meaning to meditate, cogitate, consider, think, have in mind, or hold a belief.

STEP 3: HOW WE THINK:

What is that little voice in the player's head saying? "I'm not any good!" "I'm not as good as everyone else on my team." "I'll never improve." "I have to get an athletic scholarship or I don't know what I'm going to do with my life!" "I can't help my team win with the way I play." "I'm stuck in this slump, and I can't get out of it."

Your self-perception, or thoughts, are the narrative of your life. As Henry Ford said, "Whether you think you can, or you think you can't – you're right." Essentially, thoughts determine your athlete's ability to succeed in The ATHLETE Formula; they will dictate his feelings and the ability to achieve. How you help your athlete manage his thoughts will allow him to navigate his success. The best part about thoughts is that they are your athlete's keys to accomplishment. The worst part about thoughts is that they are the ticket to your athlete's failure. Thoughts are what keep us going, help change course, or tell us to quit.

An athlete may have a lot of self-defeating thoughts running through his head, which is often referred to as "self-talk." Some self-talk is negative, such as "I'll never be any good" or "I must be the best pitcher. If I'm not the best pitcher, then I am a failure." Thoughts such as these ultimately undermine your athlete's ability to succeed. As a coach, your job is to sometimes play psychologist *(without the degree and a couch for your athlete to lie on!)*. Confront some of this self-talk. He might be thinking that he'll "never be any good." Create a more workable narrative for his self-talk, such as "If you continue working, you will get better" or "Just because you are not the best, does not mean you are not very good." *(See the CBT 101 guide in the appendix for additional information.)*

Athletes may have trouble coherently articulating these thoughts. They may be reluctant to express what they are truly thinking. Sports are designed to be challenging to the athletes. They involve testing the athlete's personal limits and having a goal of imposing his will on somebody else. Therefore, an athlete may be reluctant to admit weakness, even to a coach. Coaches need to pay attention to the athlete's words and any recurrent themes the athlete discusses. This is the window into the athlete's belief system.[7]

If the athlete seems to be focusing on themes such as being in a slump or not being able to get better at a particular skill such as shooting, then focus on the small steps, like being able to hit a

---

7   The *belief system* of a person or athlete is the set of beliefs that they have about what is right and wrong, and what is true and false.

shot from shorter distances. Say things like, "Do not worry about trying to make fifteen-foot shots right now. Just focus on trying to make five-foot shots." Work on narrowing the athlete's focus to something more achievable. Say things like, "We will work on practicing these shots so you can improve your skills." This strategy is commonly referred to as "shaping."[8]

If the athlete seems to be focusing on themes like not being as good an athlete as others on the team, my recommendation may seem counterintuitive, but there is a method to the madness. Be honest with your athlete in a similar manner that I was honest with my son, R.J. (Keep in mind that trust is important. In my situation with R.J., we have trust in each other. If you need to develop more trust with your athlete, become more task-oriented, where you specify select areas to improve upon.) If the athlete says things like, "I'm the worst player on the team. I can't do anything right. I'm not any good," your inclination may be to compliment or confront this belief system. That *might* work in some circumstances. However, in my experience, those times are few and far between. Often, when you try to convince a person that he is inaccurate, the person will double down on his belief. If the athlete is as bad as he says, then there would be no way the athlete can be convinced otherwise. In this circumstance, focus on specific areas that can be worked on to achieve improvement. Another possibility would be to provide him with other options that might bring him closer to success. Maybe he is struggling to perform properly in one position, but he might be a better fit for another position on the team. Regardless, do not be under the impression that, as a coach, you can berate an athlete to success.

---

8   *Shaping* is the process of training a learned behavior that would not normally occur. For each action closer to the desired outcome, a reinforcement or reward is provided until the target behavior is achieved.

If the athlete is not as bad as he says, then this can be a form of motivation. Regardless (and as I referenced before), an athlete is unlikely to change his opinion just from the mere fact that you, as the coach, are telling him how great he is (unless he's just fishing for compliments). This means that you are not likely to change his mind regardless of the number of compliments given. Be honest with the athlete; this helps create trust. Talk about how the athlete is not where you both want him to be, but together, you are going to work on making him better. Be sure then that you follow through to help him solve this problem; nothing hurts trust more than false promises.

Example of a "Thought" Conversation

ATHLETE: Coach, I thought about playing third base instead of shortstop like you said.

COACH: Okay, good!

ATHLETE: I tell you, Coach, I just can't get it out of my head that I have failed. It has always been my dream to play shortstop at the next level. I was told that a person should never "give up on their dreams" and "if you put your mind to something, you can accomplish anything."

COACH: You know, sometimes we achieve our dreams, but all too often, things happen and they don't quite work out the way we want them to. It is perfectly okay that we sometimes have a detour where something else happens. Often, the detour turns out to be a lot better than we thought it would be.

ATHLETE: But…

COACH: Listen, I want you to play at the next level. I think you can do that if you put in the time at third base. You might even eventually switch back to shortstop if the opportunity presents itself. However, I got a bunch of better players ahead of you on the depth chart. They have dreams, too, and I have dreams of going to the playoffs this year. I can ultimately help you develop into a really good and versatile player. This will ultimately be beneficial for you and the rest of the team if you agree to play third base for the time being.

ATHLETE: Okay…

COACH: To improve your skills, you need to gain time on the field. I'm providing you with such an opportunity. It might not look the way you thought it would, but this is a golden opportunity for you to improve.

ATHLETE: OK. I see where you are coming from. I'll play third base.

The conversation above is, of course, oversimplified. This kind of conversation may have to happen over a period of days and weeks and may not occur all at once. Telling a goal-driven athlete that he may struggle to achieve his goals might be very hard for him to hear. Also, you may not be the ideal individual to have this kind of conversation with him. It's possible that someone such as another coach, whom he has a better relationship with, might be able to converse with him better. The athlete might have a better rapport with this person. Have this other coach try to deliver the message.

Another strategy is to discuss how the athlete is not very good at some things, but there are other things that he can do to help the team. As an example, if the athlete is not good at shooting, tell him that for right now, he should focus on rebounding, playing good defense, and boxing out to help the team; those activities are more based on effort and less on skill. If the athlete engages in those effort-based activities, this will help increase his playing time. Having more playing time can help increase his confidence (more on confidence later) and will give him more opportunities to take risks and engage in more skill-based activities like shooting. This can be a pivotal point for your coach-athlete relationship. This could easily be the tipping point in your athlete's career to determine if he further develops or if he plateaus.

CHANGING HOW WE THINK: The Failure and Success of Mariano Rivera

One of my favorite examples to prove this point is that of Hall of Fame relief pitcher Mariano Rivera. Rivera was not a highly ranked prospect as he was starting his professional career. He was underwhelming as a starting pitcher and suffered from some injuries. After some stints in the minor leagues, Rivera was ultimately "demoted" to the bullpen. The demotion was the greatest thing that ever happened to him. All Rivera did in the bullpen was become the greatest relief pitcher in baseball history and first-ballot Hall of Fame player. Did Rivera achieve his goal of becoming a starting pitcher? No, he did not. However, Rivera had to change his thoughts so that he did not view being a relief pitcher as a failure but as a new, unplanned opportunity to succeed.

The whole goal of The ATHLETE Formula is to help you improve your coaching of athletes. The ATHLETE Formula's goal is to give you tools to help them improve their performance and/or bounce back following adversity by incorporating mental strategies. However, keep in mind all those clichés such as "If you put your mind to something, you can accomplish anything." Who told you that lie? It's not true. Whoever told you that lie is doing you and your athletes a disservice! It's ridiculous. Putting your mind to something can help you succeed in *some* REALISTIC areas. If I keep practicing my running, I will invariably run faster. I will never make the Olympics at my ripe old age, but if I trained hard enough and long enough, I could increase my speed and maybe complete a marathon. The goal of The ATHLETE Formula is to help coach your athletes to improve their skills. Just keep in mind that there might be physical and situational factors that prevent players from achieving that ultimate goal. Many people never achieve their *ultimate* goal despite their best efforts. Do not let perfect be the enemy of good. Often, athletes become so focused on being perfect that they miss out on trying the opportunities that come with improvement and getting good at something.

The athlete's thoughts allow him to keep pursuing opportunities and put him in the best position to succeed. One common type of thought an athlete might have is "Why is this taking so long to achieve my goal?" Work with the athlete to change his thinking to something like "I am going to have to spend more time on the basic skills if I want to ultimately succeed." Also, his thoughts allow him to be open to new opportunities, which might give him a better chance to succeed. Often, the greatest path to achievement is continuing to work on your skills and waiting for new opportunities (or what sometimes looks like a demotion) to develop. Mariano Rivera is an extreme example. Help your athletes be mindful and open to new and different opportunities that may be related to the goal but not the original goal that they had in mind. This new goal may ultimately be a better situation and open him up to new areas of opportunity. There are plenty of stories about athletes who lacked the requisite athletic talents in one area but parlayed that into something else.

Ultimately, athletes (*or anyone for that matter*) do not change because of their thoughts. While the thoughts are a necessary start, the athlete's emotions are going to be his ultimate driver.

42

CHAPTER 6

LIVING WITH EMOTIONS

The fourth step in The ATHLETE Formula is the "Living with Emotions" step. Emotions are how we feel in response to our thoughts. Success is often predicated on how well we properly manage our emotions.

> The definition of "emotion" is a strong feeling. This word dates back to 1579 and has its roots in a French word meaning to "stir up."

STEP 4: LIVING WITH EMOTIONS

What emotions or feelings are you experiencing as a result of that little voice in your head? Does the athlete get "anxious" when he does things such as going to the free-throw line? Is he "frustrated" because he cannot hit that ball off the tee? Is he "jealous" because another athlete was picked to start instead of him?

So let me be frank. This is likely going to be the biggest challenge. We are dealing with humans and not robots; the athlete is going to have emotions. Emotions dictate decisions more than anything else. Don't believe me? Ever yell at your spouse, kid, or dog after a frustrating day at work? Logically, you know that they did not do anything to harm you, but you are looking for an outlet to express your frustration with various forms of anger, such as yelling at others or banging your hand on the table. When you cannot get out of bed in the morning to exercise (something very healthy), these are your emotions screaming at you. Some of these emotions may include fatigue, irritability, or lethargy. I often have clients complain to me that people in their lives are illogical. Of course, people are illogical and base their decisions on emotions. Have you ever grabbed a Coca-Cola over water? You know water is healthier and less expensive! Have you ever eaten at a fast-food restaurant because it is easy and you do not feel like cooking? Don't you know that eating at home is usually better for you? All the information in the world does not usually change our course of action. We want to quickly FEEL better, and we do everything we can do to provide ourselves with the feelings we desire, even if it is ultimately undermining our future.

Dealing with Emotions: Pitcher Jon Lester Cannot Throw a Ball

Jon Lester was one of the best pitchers in baseball for nearly a decade. He was an all-star and an ace pitcher. Lester was instrumental in helping the Chicago Cubs and Boston Red Sox win the World Series. He had a large repertoire of pitches he could throw and got the best hitters in baseball out. There was not much Lester could not do on the pitching mound, except for one thing. For much of Jon Lester's career, he experienced anxiety about throwing the ball to first base. He went years in between throws to first base. Runners would take tremendous leads off first base, and he would never throw over there. If a batter bunted the ball, he was useless. Usually, the catcher or third baseman would have to field the ball. If he happened to field a ground ball, Lester would typically have to run with the ball toward first base so he could make a less anxiety-provoking, short, underhand toss to the first baseman.

Lester never truly resolved this difficulty. He did work with his coaches to devise techniques where he occasionally threw to first base from the pitcher's mound.

Often, when dealing with emotions such as anxiety, depression, and fear, the key is to devise modified strategies and techniques to help you deal with such difficulties. This is part of the reason I said that this might be the most difficult part to resolve. Emotions can cause even the best athletes to behave illogically. Emotions, unfortunately, can override any level of intelligence. As this scenario shows, one of the best pitchers in baseball was unable to accomplish a simple act that a nine-year-old child could do. However, a coach's job is to accept the athlete's emotions as they are and then create strategies and methods that help him manage his emotions on the playing field.

The athlete's emotions must be acknowledged but are sometimes distractions from what he wants to accomplish. Acknowledge their existence. Emotions need to be accounted for whether we like them or not. Think about what the athlete might be feeling. Listen to his words; the feelings may be intertwined with the thoughts. Often, emotions can be harder to articulate. Sometimes, all an athlete might say is that he feels" mad" or "angry."[9] There is another emotion behind that feeling of being "mad" or "angry." It is vital to figure out the root emotion that he is experiencing. He might have trouble articulating; try to help him the best you can. Is he feeling depressed? Frustrated? Overwhelmed by the circumstances?

---

9   The emotions "mad" or "angry" are considered secondary emotions. There is always a primary emotion behind the anger such as frustration, anxiety, or fatigue. It is important to seek out the primary emotion.

Whatever he is feeling is inherently fine, and a person is not weak because of it. Some of the more common feelings he might experience are sadness, depression, anxiety, being overwhelmed, frustration, or jealousy (refer to the list of other common feelings in the quick guide at the end of this chapter). Try to listen to his words and validate or paraphrase them. Maybe the athlete is talking to you and you say something like, "Wow! You sound very frustrated because you are struggling to hit the ball." He may agree with your assessment, or he may not. If he does not, listen some more and try to paraphrase something else. When you hit the nail on the head, the athlete will likely acknowledge it.

Do not put words in his mouth. Do not say something like, "I think you're really upset because I didn't start you today." He might agree with you because you are the coach and the athlete might think, "I must listen to my coach." There is a power differential between coach and athlete. The athlete could be upset at something completely unrelated to your coaching decision. He could be upset about something that happened at home or that he was turned down for a scholarship at his dream school.

When trying to talk with your athletes, keep in mind that part of their reluctance may be due to their defense mechanisms,[10] which are typically normal and healthy. In sports, defense mechanisms will help an athlete who strikes out say, "I'll get him next time," or they can help an athlete who is going through a slump tell himself that he'll work harder to get out of it. However, defense mechanisms become problematic when they interfere with a person's physical and mental functioning. An athlete may develop a cognitive

---

10 *Defense mechanisms* are unconscious psychological processes employed to defend against feelings of anxiety and unacceptable impulses at the level of consciousness.

distortion[11] instead of facing reality. An athlete may become rigid and unwilling to make adjustments or ask for help. Some examples of defense mechanisms include the following:

DENIAL: A refusal to accept reality; the athlete may refuse to perceive it or deny that it exists.

> EXAMPLE: *The athlete claims to be the best hitter on the team despite having mediocre statistics.*

REPRESSION: Often referred to as "motivated forgetting"; the athlete is unable to recall a threatening situation, person, or event.

> EXAMPLE: *The athlete claims that tonight's starting pitcher has never been able to get him out; in actuality, the athlete has gone two for ten against this pitcher, including five strikeouts.*

PROJECTION: Attributing one's own unwanted thoughts, feelings, and motives to someone else; the athlete sees his own unacceptable attributes in others.

> EXAMPLE: *The athlete claims that he is getting reduced playing time because the coach does not like him. In actuality, the athlete does not like the coach, so he shows up late to practice and does not give his best effort during games.*

DISPLACEMENT: The redirection of an often aggressive impulse onto a powerless substitute target; the athlete may take out his frustrations for not playing well on weaker teammates or family members.

> EXAMPLE: *The starting quarterback blames all the team's failures and shortcomings on his lesser-skilled teammates.*

---

11 *Cognitive distortion* is an exaggerated or irrational thought pattern involved in the onset or perpetuation of psychopathological states, such as depression and anxiety. Cognitive distortions are thoughts that cause individuals to perceive reality inaccurately.

RATIONALIZATION: A cognitive distortion or exaggeration of "the facts" to make an event or impulse less threatening; the athlete might provide certain excuses for his lack of performance.

EXAMPLE: The starting pitcher gave up six runs in the first inning. He claims that this would have never happened except for the fact that his personal catcher was injured and could not play that day.

REACTION FORMATION: Behaving in the opposite way that you think or feel; the athlete may try to overcompensate for a thought or emotion.

EXAMPLE: The starting pitcher has a sprained ankle and cannot properly push off the mound. However, he says, "I feel great and am ready to go. I can go nine innings today with no problem!"

Example of an "Emotion" Conversation

COACH: Hey! Are you doing okay? You don't seem like yourself lately.

ATHLETE: I'm okay. I just need to get back to practice. We've got a big game this weekend, and I need to be ready.

COACH: You sure?

ATHLETE: No, I'm good, Coach. There's nothing talking can do to solve this. I need to get back on the field and play my game.

COACH: Maybe I can help you out or give you some suggestions. Sometimes, talking it out a bit can at least make you feel better. I've been through a lot and have seen a lot. This old man might be able to help you.

ATHLETE: I'm okay, Coach. Words aren't going to help me hit a fastball.

COACH: Tell you what. Why don't you go to practice now and maybe swing by my office in the morning and we can have some coffee and talk before classes?

(The next morning at 7 a.m. in the coach's office)

ATHLETE: Good morning, Coach.

COACH: Hey, buddy! I've known you since you were a freshman. I know when something is bothering you. It's okay. Whatever you say stays between us.

ATHLETE: So…um… I want to play college baseball. I love baseball and playing baseball is my only ticket to pay for school. I have not received any scholarship offers. My best friend on the team, Joe, the third baseman, has gotten three offers from Division 1-A schools. Joe does not need the money. His dad is loaded. Mine is not.

COACH: So it sounds like you're frustrated that you are not getting offers and jealous that Joe has all these opportunities that you do not have.

ATHLETE: You could say that.

COACH: That's understandable. I have had a lot of players over the years, me included, who have had to go in through the back door to achieve success, like you.

ATHLETE: Really?

COACH: Let me see what I can do to help you. Guys like us often must take the road less traveled to become successful! Haha!

ATHLETE: Okay! Thanks, Coach!

COACH: Now get to class. I'll see you at practice later.

This is another scenario that occurs within the coach's office. One strategy that sometimes helps is to not be in such a formal setting, like an office, when these conversations occur. Talk while playing catch, shooting baskets, or going for a walk. While eye contact is usually important when engaging in conversation, often too much eye contact in a difficult or emotional conversation can be intimidating to some. Create a less formal environment. Also, when talking to someone, don't immediately go for the main topic of discussion. Try some small talk on some other less threatening topic first; small talk can be annoying because we just want to "get to the point and move on." Unfortunately, small talk in a less formal environment is sometimes a necessary step to drive the conversation productively.

Once the emotion seems pinned down, think about ways the athlete can reconcile these emotions. Help the athlete become honest with himself and you. This is not easy. Good athletes are trained to persevere through the most difficult of athletic circumstances. However, maybe it is as simple as removing him from playing for a little while. Maybe the athlete just wants to talk or cry a little bit. It is possible that it might be as simple as a few short breaths and a drink of water to do the trick. However, it could be something that will take longer and is more involved. Maybe there is something going on at home that is making the emotional part of sports more difficult. Regardless, give him an opportunity to deal with his feelings. This could mean talking, or it could mean needing some solitude. It does not matter; let him reconcile these emotions in a way that feels most comfortable. The athlete might be more comfortable talking things through with a trusted teammate or another coach. He might also want to talk with you in private, away from the playing field. The athlete might do better articulating his feelings through writing.

If you and your athlete are having difficulty discussing and/or identifying emotions, that is understandable. It is often hard to put words to emotions, but it is important. I have included a MOOD METER of many common emotions.

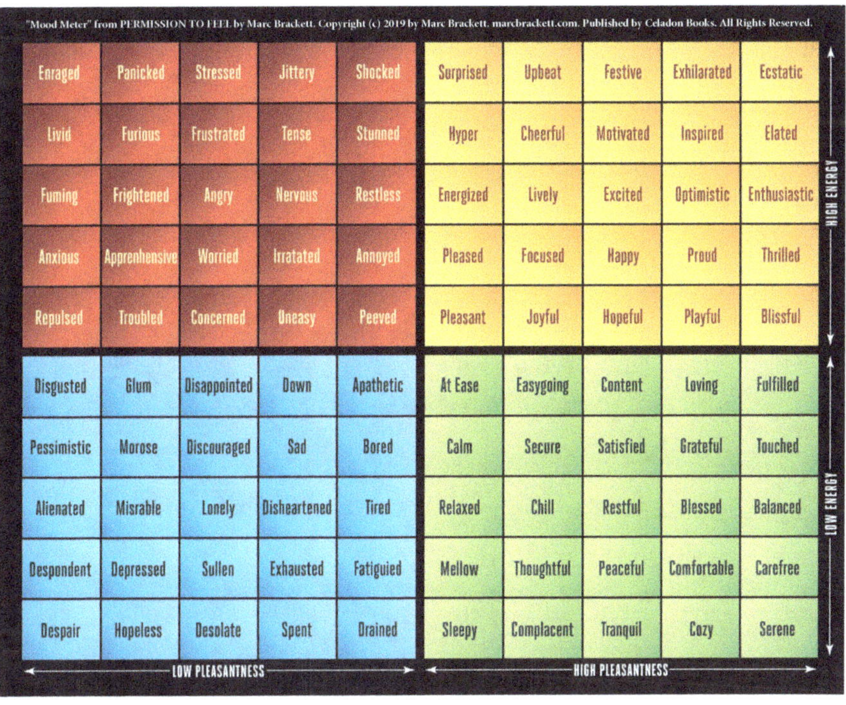

The ATHLETE Formula

CHAPTER 7

EXUDING CONFIDENCE

The fifth step in The ATHLETE Formula is "Exuding Confidence." Confidence is a feeling of self-assurance arising from a person's appreciation of their own abilities or qualities. When an athlete is going through difficult times, confidence is the gasoline of his resilience.

> The definition of "**confidence**" is the belief in yourself and your powers or abilities. It is derived from Latin and means to trust completely.

STEP 5: EXUDING CONFIDENCE

What are small changes in thoughts, emotions, and/or behaviors you can help your athlete make to build his confidence? My athlete is not as skilled as others; what can he still do things to help the team? He is not a starter, but I want to develop him to be the best possible backup. My athlete may be having trouble making his shots today, but I want him to work on helping others score.

If emotions are going to be the toughest challenge, then confidence is going to be a close second. Confidence is a complex and multifaceted idea; your athlete needs to have confidence to become successful, but it is hard to have confidence in the absence of success. There is some overlap between confidence, thoughts, and emotions. One of the elements that differentiates confidence is that it helps keep an athlete going during difficult times. In essence, confidence is a believable narrative we have of ourselves. It is easy to have false confidence when things are going well and a lack of confidence when things are not going well. The difficulty is stabilizing confidence during good and bad times.

The first part of confidence is building it up when there is no track record of accomplishment. Think of the book The Little Engine That Could (Platt & Munk, 1930). The little engine had to go up a mountain while carrying freight, and he had to constantly say to himself, "I think I can. I think I can." When pursuing an endeavor, an athlete may lack any real evidence that he can eventually succeed. However, it is important to help him build resiliency and engage in mental preparation, as this will be a prolonged process to achieve the goal.

The second part of confidence is maintaining it and/or bouncing back when in a slump. Being in a slump is one of the most emotionally taxing things an athlete can go through. Trying something new is difficult; however, trying to become successful at something that you have already succeeded at but can no longer achieve for no apparent reason can be baffling. The athlete often has a natural tendency to try to push harder and impose his will on the situation. There is a tendency to want to do things like swing more intensely or throw harder or take more difficult shots. Unfortunately, such tendencies tend to hamper the athlete's performance, cause him to feel more frustrated, and put him into an even deeper slump.

As you try to help the athlete build his confidence, his negative emotions often creep in. Some of the common emotions an athlete will feel when things are not going well include frustration, discouragement, and/or despair. These commonly occur when the athlete is not experiencing the success he had anticipated or the process is going slower than expected.

When emotions such as these begin occurring while an athlete is training, this is often a sign that he needs to pause (notice I did not say "stop") the training. Take a break for at least a few hours, or maybe even until the next day. When he becomes frustrated, he could unintentionally do things to undermine his own success. If he is engaging in activities such as putting a golf ball or shooting a free throw, the elevated heart rate, the tightening of the hands, and the increase in sweat all make it harder to succeed. Try pausing the activity and do something relaxing or fun! The athlete is not being productive, and negative thoughts and emotions are only impairments to his sense of confidence.

Negative thoughts impede an athlete's resilience. Common negative thoughts can include "When will I finally get out of this?" or "This is going to last forever!" These negative thoughts fuel more negative feelings, which can often cause athletes to do things improperly (i.e., throw harder, swing harder) at the expense of proven sports fundamental practices. Veering away from such fundamentals will likely result in more discouragement, self-doubt, and feeling demoralized.

At this point, have him relax and engage in another activity completely unrelated to the task he is practicing. To give this enough time, pause the task for AT LEAST twenty minutes and no more than a day.[12] Depending on how he is feeling at the time, he might need a break from all athletic activities. Tell him to sit on the bench for a little while to cool off if needed. This will give him time to lower his heart rate, stop sweating, and stop those negative thoughts and emotions by engaging in another less frustrating activity or through relaxation.

Do not encourage the athlete to be tough and push through this difficulty. Of course, everybody has read stories about a superstar, a famous athlete who shot a thousand free throws per day when he was growing up, and the guy who swung the golf clubs until his knuckles bled and he still pushed through. It is highly unlikely that this happened in such a manner. Adults also like to tell stories about walking to school uphill both ways in the snow with no shoes. Be careful about falling for this mythology. Nonetheless, even if that worked for one person, it does not work for most athletes. If the goal is to improve the athlete's performance, then that is what The ATHLETE Formula is for. If your goal is to tell tall tales to your friends and family, then sign up for a creative writing class.

A big take-home message of this is that when your athlete is struggling, pull back a little first, just for now; have him do less

---

12 Why was the suggestion made to keep it between twenty minutes and the next day? Is there something magical about that period of time? According to Rossi, E. L., & Nimmons, D. (1991), in *The 20-Minute Break: Reduce Stress, Maximize Performance, and Improve Health and Emotional Well-Being Using the New Science of Ultradian Rhythms*. (No Title) shows the benefits of performance on various tasks when given about a twenty-minute break. The next day was recommended on the high end because, depending on how emotional an athlete is, he might need a full day of rest before returning to the stress-inducing activity. The basic premise is that the athlete should return to the activity within a finite period instead of "when I get around to it." At that point, it will likely never happen.

and NOT more! This constant pushing an athlete well beyond his limits to the point of causing him emotional and physical pain is detrimental to his confidence and resiliency because of the reinforcement of poor performance. Confidence is the only thing that can keep an athlete going when faced with a difficult activity. A coach constantly yelling at him will not typically achieve such results.

KEY CONCEPTS OF CONFIDENCE

LEARNED HELPLESSNESS: A state that occurs after a person has experienced a stressful situation repeatedly. They come to believe that they are unable to control or change the situation, so they do not try—even when opportunities for change become available. Often, people think their learned helplessness is permanent, pervasive, and personal. If an athlete is struggling, he might experience learned helplessness. As his coach, help him realize that this is temporary, limited, and should not be taken personally. The struggle is simply a difficulty that can be worked through and can be overcome.

STRESS INOCULATION: Training that aims to help a person cope better with stress so it doesn't further impact their physical or mental health or, in the athlete's case, his performance. Help him prepare for stressful situations before they happen. As a coach, you can help your athlete engage in stress inoculation to help him understand his stressors and develop stress management skills. This goes beyond practicing a skill like getting better at shooting free throws or hitting a ball. You, as the coach, are helping the athlete work through his stressful feelings in a safe environment, like while practicing. Keep in mind that you are not just practicing a skill but the interface between skill and confidence.

Remember how earlier I said to "pause"? That's precisely what I mean. The athlete needs to pause and not stop and give up. Often, if the pause is prolonged, the athlete becomes disheartened and discouraged and gives up because the activity appears too difficult. No improvement occurs without any practice. Therefore, the pause in the activity must be temporary. You and your athlete should choose a date and time when this activity will resume. You are simply allowing him to regroup and return somewhere between twenty minutes and the next day.

Having feelings such as frustration and discouragement are normal. Part of the reason he may be experiencing these feelings is that the bar that was set may be too high. If this is the case, expectations can be adjusted to something temporarily less challenging. In order not to lose confidence, the athlete needs to feel some level of success. Again, confidence is the only thing that will keep an athlete going in the face of failure.

Another issue having to do with confidence is when an athlete is in a slump, loses confidence, and struggles in an area where he used to be successful. Slumps happen, and when they do, it is important not to become a prisoner of the moment. He might say, "I'll never get out of this." Pay attention to this as a "thought" (see Step 3). This might diminish his confidence because he can see no improvement in sight. Another problematic thing the athlete might say is "I've got to get out of this." The issue here is that it puts undue pressure on him. Athletes tend to begin to do counterproductive things, such as tightening their hands on a bat or a club or throwing a ball harder than it should be thrown out of frustration.

Sometimes, athletes start getting tunnel vision and become unwilling to listen to the coach's advice. Athletes often want to do more and overexert themselves, which ends up prolonging their slump. Sometimes it helps to view a slump like an injury. You might need to help the athlete make alterations in his tactics while recovering.

Example of a "Confidence" Conversation

COACH: Hey! You seem like you are struggling with your hitting right now.

ATHLETE: Coach, I can't seem to hit anything right now. I can't recall when I got my last hit.

COACH: I've been watching what you've been doing. Players will go through slumps from time to time, but there are things players sometimes do that make things worse. They get away from their fundamentals. Players like you start swinging harder and tightening their hands more than they normally would.

ATHLETE: Coach, I'm just so frustrated! I want to get out of this slump! I'm trying everything, and nothing is working!

COACH: Well, that is part of your problem!!

ATHLETE: What's that?

COACH: You are trying "everything." You don't need to try everything to get out of your slump. You need to work on getting back to your fundamentals. I'll also look at your swing more closely. I'll see if you might be doing something with your hands or your stance that could be causing you some problems.

ATHLETE: Thanks, Coach!

COACH: Again, I know you're frustrated, but for starters, don't swing harder and don't tighten your hands. Also, don't say, "I want to get out of this slump." Say to yourself, "I'm going to work on getting out of this slump." This at least puts you on the right path to help get you out of this tough time.

ATHLETE: Thanks, Coach!

Often, in sports, athletes default to using strength to resolve a situation. They try to push harder to impose their will on another human or circumstance. Unfortunately, this often results in the tightening of muscles, getting away from fundamentals, and doing other things that lead to poorer results. When trying to bounce back, focus more on technique and style. Putting less emphasis on sheer force will usually improve performance. Such techniques also build confidence and help an athlete endure difficulties.

The first thing an athlete needs to do is change his self-talk by saying things like "I will find a way out of this" or "I'm going to have to figure out some new strategies to fix this." Using self-talk like this is a good first step in building confidence. The athlete is acknowledging that there is a problem and is expressing that he understands he is going to take time to work at fixing it. However, the self-talk is also telling the athlete that change is within HIS control. Letting the athlete know that he has control is an important part of confidence-building. Once the athlete thinks that he has no control over his circumstances, his chances of success become more difficult. When all is going well, it is easy to have confidence. However, trying to maintain a level of confidence is imperative when an athlete is not achieving his desired results. What is a believable narrative he can tell himself that will help him be resilient during difficult times?

Even the Best Can Be in a Slump

Alex Bregman only seems to know success. He was the second pick in the MLB draft, an All-Star, and a World Series champion. When he was called up by the Houston Astros as a rookie, he wanted to make a big splash in the major leagues. Alex certainly made a big splash, just not the kind of splash he was hoping for. He was hitless in his first seventeen major league at-bats. Throughout about thirty at-bats, he only had one hit. It was probably not the way he was hoping to start his major league career. He spoke later in an interview and said that this difficult stretch was not only hard on him, but it was also difficult on his family.

However, while we only think about Alex's successes, Alex remembered some of his failures. He recalled slumps and setbacks he had in high school and college. Alex drew from his failures (not successes) and developed a pattern of self-talk where he told himself he knew he could get out of the slump; he would take this difficult early period of his career and use it as a way to have a successful major league career.

These steps are the prerequisite to what you, as the coach, and the athlete can now tackle in the next chapter.

62

CHAPTER 8

TACTICS

The sixth step in The ATHLETE Formula is the "Tactics" step. Tactics is a process of changing patterns of human behavior using motivational techniques to achieve a more desirable outcome. This is the appreciable goal of coaching.

The definition of "Tactics" is an action or strategy carefully planned to achieve a specific end. "Tactics" comes from a Greek word meaning "the art of arrangement."

STEP 6: TACTICS

How are you going to help your athlete execute improved performance? The ultimate goal is to have the athlete engage in an action that improves his results, like hitting a ball more regularly or having the ball go in the basket more consistently. One common strategy might be to have your athlete temporarily engage in an easier or simplified version of the task to improve upon and help him bounce back from a difficult period. Another technique is to use stress inoculation and find short relaxation techniques an athlete can use in the moment on the playing field (see the Quick Guide in the Appendix for some suggestions). Another idea is to have the athlete in a backup role but still be responsible for making sure the starter is properly prepared. This can help him learn vicariously through the starter's experiences.

In some respects, Tactics can work similarly and in parallel to Confidence. This may seem a bit counterintuitive, but one of the keys to the Tactics step when the athlete is struggling is to start by doing *less* action. If the athlete is struggling from a lack of skill, lack of confidence, or is in a slump, then the LAST thing the coach should have the athlete do is more. When we are toddlers, our parents work on the basics of the alphabet and counting. Parents do not give the toddler a thesis to write or trigonometry to figure out. It is too much and is overwhelming. Success would be impossible for the child because of a lack of skill. As the child continues to struggle, his confidence diminishes and ultimately, does not obtain the necessary tools for success. Your athletes are no different. Coaches may need to break down skills into steps in a similar manner.

If your athlete is showing signs of being overwhelmed with a situation, reduce the steps to their essence. Work on one step at a time. Your athlete may look big and strong, but learning or bouncing back is the same regardless of age or build. If a second baseman is trying to better turn a double-play, this involves many smaller steps that need to happen one at a time: a) he needs to run to second base and get his feet and hands in the correct position; b) he needs to catch the ball from the shortstop; c) he has to move his feet properly to be in position to make a good, strong throw to first base; and lastly, d) he needs to make a strong and accurate throw to first base. One way to accomplish this is first working on Step A until it has been mastered, then progressing to Step B until that is mastered, then combining Steps A and B until they can be done fluidly. Then, work on Step C and incorporate that into Steps A and B. Finally, work on Step D and work that into Steps A, B, and C.

Have you ever injured your arm or leg and had to rehabilitate it? What did you do? You engaged in simple exercises (meaning, simple if you're not injured) to try to build your strength to where it needed to be. Thoughts, emotions, and/or confidence are the same way. A person engages in simple tasks to build up their thoughts, emotions, and/or confidence muscles. Too often, people err on the side of doing more. That is simply illogical. If you're rehabilitating from a broken ankle, would you *START* by running a marathon? Of course not. You would start by taking simple steps with the goal of at least beginning to walk again. The marathon will eventually come.

So, the activity you will engage your athlete in obviously depends on the sport and what he is struggling with. However, let me give you a few suggestions, and you can tailor it as needed. While you are engaging in action, be mindful that we are looking for behavioral improvement but not perfection.

Keep in mind not to let perfect be the enemy of good. Perfection is unattainable. Even the greatest athletes never achieve absolute perfection. They are always finding ways to "improve" their craft.

ACTION STEP STRATEGIES

Shaping and Stress Inoculation:

A situation when *shaping* can help is when the athlete is struggling with free-throw shooting and wants to get better; the struggle can be the result of a lack of skill or that he is in a slump. The free-throw line is fifteen feet from the basket. Move him up five feet or to where he is ten feet from the basket. Go through his same free-throw routine while being closer to the basket. If ten feet is still too far for him, then move him up a few more feet until he can consistently[13] make the shot. After he can consistently make the shot from where you are, move back one or two feet. That's a slightly more difficult shot, so the athlete may not be able to make this shot as consistently at first; it might take some practice. Eventually, he will hit that shot consistently.

After that shot is made consistently, move back another one or two feet. Continue the process until he gets to the true free-throw line.[14] As the athlete demonstrates incremental improvement, be sure to take note and say something positive. No need to go over the top, but acknowledge with statements that might include "Good job," "You're on the right track," "You're getting it," or "You're improving, and that's what counts." Do not ever put a time frame on this improvement. Each athlete is different. Do not say something like, "Okay, we are going to do this shaping, and I need you set to go by Saturday's game." This is an improvement process and not one with a defined finish line.

Here is how shaping can be implemented:

Shaping

The process of establishing a behavior that is not learned or performed by an individual who is present is referred to as Shaping.

---

13 Consistency can mean different things to different people. It's rare that anybody can reach 100% consistency on anything. Consistency is very personal and task specific. A good free-throw shooter hits 80% of his shots and a good baseball player gets a hit 30% of the time. Therefore, I will recommend consistency as a rate that one is content with.

14 This is something that might take multiple days to achieve. For example, an athlete might take several days to consistently make a shot from a given distance.

Shaping can also be defined as reinforcing behaviors that are closer to the target behavior, also known as successive approximations. This technique serves a dual purpose. It helps improve an athlete's skill AND his confidence. Nothing increases confidence like developing a successful track record of performance improvement.

- For starters, reinforce any behavior that is even remotely close to the desired target behavior.

- The next step is to reinforce the behavior that is closer to the target behavior. Also, don't reinforce the previous behavior.

- Keep reinforcing the responses/behaviors that resemble the target behavior even more closely. Continue reinforcing the successive approximations until the target behavior is achieved.

- Once the target behavior is achieved, only reinforce the final response.

Stress Inoculation

Stress Inoculation is something that can also be used with shaping techniques. If possible, while practicing, try to mimic a true game situation. During the game, the athlete might experience things such as heightened anxiety from the noise of the crowd, the referees, the clock, and other players around him. Try to bring as much of that environment as you can to your practice. If possible, have family, friends, players, or spectators stand on either side of the painted area. Play music or loud crowd noise. Have people yelling things at the athlete. This creates a high-pressure situation that the player has to overcome.[15] Have the athlete pay attention to what

---

15 "There are three seconds left in the game. He is at the free-throw line. One successful free throw will tie the game and two successful free throws will win the game."

his body is doing. Is he sweating more? Is his heart rate elevated? In this high-pressure situation, is he shooting the ball harder, and is he expediting your free throw routine? Try to figure out ways for the athlete to relax when these physical symptoms occur. Some common strategies include taking slow breaths, closing his eyes for a short period, saying something calming to himself, and having a routine when the athlete heads to the free-throw line like bouncing the ball five times before shooting. All these things and more can be contributing factors to why he is struggling. Sports is often a game of inches. Small movements can have dramatic impacts on your performance.

Along similar lines but in a different sport, when playing golf, there are several things you can also do to help your athlete when building up a skill or trying to defeat a slump. When putting, do not have your athlete try hitting the ball twenty feet from the hole. I have heard of a golf pro who trains his students to just try to hit the ball in from three feet away for starters to build confidence and success. If three feet is too far for starters or while in a slump, the pro will move the ball in closer if necessary. Another golf scenario might be when an athlete is struggling when teeing off. Encourage him to practice by just working on the direction and not distance. Focus on him getting the ball onto the fairway consistently. After the athlete can comfortably get the ball on the fairway, he should gradually look to add slightly more power and distance to the shot. These are strategies used in shaping, which is an effective method because it is helpful in an athlete's thoughts, emotions, and/or confidence and is instrumental in the ACTION step.

- RELAXATION: Relaxation can take on multiple forms in the ACTION step. The first one is "stress inoculation," which was already discussed. One technique to help the athlete relax may involve working with him to develop a routine or comforting ritual before he takes a free throw. Another method would be to engage in a relaxation technique, such as taking two long and slow breaths to slightly lower their anxiety. For some athletes, it helps to visualize what they are going to do. Others may want to engage in self-affirming talk. All these planned methods of relaxation can be part of the training process.

Sometimes, in the heat of a difficult and high-anxiety situation, a coach and/or an athlete can implement some quick techniques to help reduce tension. Maybe you can say something funny to break the stress or tell your athletes to think of something funny, pleasant, or relaxing. This can include having the athlete tell himself a joke.

KEEP IT AWAY FROM THE GOAT

Legendary NBA coach Phil Jackson was once calling a game-winning shot for his team, the Chicago Bulls. He sensed the team was tense and jokingly said to keep the ball away from the Bulls' best player, arguably the greatest player ever, Michael Jordan. The players reported later that this attempt at humor helped calm their nerves and contributed to the success of that final play.

THE CANDY MAN CAN

During a game-winning drive in the Super Bowl, San Francisco 49ers quarterback Joe Montana noticed that one of his teammates was tense and pointed out that actor John Candy was in the stands. This helped calm this player, and the 49ers scored a touchdown in what was the game-winning drive.

These distractions help relieve some people's levels of tension and anxiety and allow them to perform better. Everybody's situation is going to be different. Experiment with what works best to help your athletes relax. Here are some examples.

Progressive Muscle Relaxation:

- Have the athlete start by sitting or lying down. He should take a breath and squeeze one group of muscles at a time, perhaps starting with his feet. He should hold his breath for five to ten seconds. Then, as the athlete breathes out, he can relax those muscles for ten to twenty seconds. Now, he can move on to the next muscle group. He should repeat the exercise until he hits most of the muscles in his body.

Box Breathing:

- Have the athlete breathe in slowly for four counts.
- Tell him to breathe in for four counts and then exhale.
- Instruct him to breathe out slowly for four counts.
- Have him hold his breath for four counts.
- (Repeat as necessary)

Be Mindful for One Minute:

- Work with your athlete to develop mindfulness. This is a type of meditation where the athlete focuses only on the here and now. Research shows that mindfulness can decrease worry and stress. This can be done during almost any activity.

Listen to Music:

- Tell the athlete to listen to his favorite tunes that he finds relaxing. This can help him bounce back more quickly from stress.

Rethink Posture:

- Body language says a lot about your athlete's mood. When your athlete has negative emotions, his posture often collapses. The shoulders round, causing slouching. This position can keep those tough feelings hanging around. To help let them go, have the athlete simply sit or stand taller.

Practice Cue-Controlled Relaxation:

- Have your athlete start by thinking of a word (or phrase) that he associates with deep relaxation. Maybe it's "peace" or "beach." Once he has chosen his word, have him start breathing deeply. As he breathes out, have him say the word. Have him repeat it until he feels relaxed. Over time, his body and mind will begin to relax as soon as he says the cue word. He should start to feel better even faster.

Move the Body:

- It's no secret that exercise can be a stress reliever. But your athlete can get benefits without having to take a fitness class or go for a run. Just moving his body for a minute or two can help. Have him take a quick stroll around the block or do some simple stretches. Turn on some tunes and dance.

CHAPTER 9

EVALUATE YOUR LEGACY

I f you have successfully brought your athlete through the paces as described in this program, he now has the skills that were lacking before. He can hit a ball better, catch a ball better, or throw a ball better. That's it! The ATHLETE Formula is now over!!

Not really! There is a seventh step.

The definition of "legacy" is anything handed down from the past, as from a predecessor. Legacy comes from a Latin word that means "ambassador" or "a body of persons sent on a mission." Consider yourself a kind of ambassador who is on a mission.

STEP 7: EVALUATE YOUR LEGACY

This is what The ATHLETE Formula is all about. Pass the skills and the process on to your athletes and other coaches. Kobe Bryant developed a "Mamba Mentality" to help himself. He then passed this ideology on to others. You pass The ATHLETE Formula knowledge on to others. This is very important on two levels. The first is that one of the best ways to retain and improve certain skills is to teach them to others. However, more importantly, this is how a coach leaves an imprint that goes well beyond points and home runs.

You have now completed The ATHLETE Formula, and you now know how to improve your athlete's performance. Take this and go use it on an athlete and/or find a coach who is confused, frustrated, struggling, or overwhelmed with his athletes and impart this knowledge to him. No championship ring will ever feel as satisfying as doing that. Do you ever listen to Hall of Fame speeches where people thank their small-town high school football coach? That can be you, too. Maybe the person you help does not make it to Cooperstown, but maybe you help lift someone to where he landed an athletic scholarship that resulted in his being able to go to college and get into a coaching role. Maybe he came from a difficult home life and the sport you coached him on became a productive outlet for him. You simply do not know. So work to be in an athlete's personal Hall of Fame speech, which will make you a legend in his eyes.

PLANTING TREES and CREATING PATHS

Pete Jacobson was an inconsistent wrestler during much of his high school career. However, he received proper encouragement from his coach at the time, which propelled him to wrestle in college, and then he became a highly successful high school coach.

In professional and college-level sports, sometimes people discuss coaching trees. Like a family tree, it outlines the relationship of coaches and who influenced them. It typically outlines a noteworthy head coach and who some of his assistant coaches were. Those assistant coaches eventually became head coaches. Paths can be drawn to demonstrate philosophical influence and legacy.

One of the most prominent coaching trees is that of Bill Walsh, who was, most notably, the head coach of the San Francisco 49ers in the 1980s and led them to three Super Bowl championships. As successful as he was as a coach, his legacy stands the test of time. Six of Bill Walsh's assistant coaches went on to become head coaches. To date, of those six assistant coaches who became head coaches, twenty-five of their assistants also ended up becoming head coaches. Bill Walsh was not just great himself; he helped other coaches become successful, too.

In the same way that Pete Jacobson's coach created a path for him and Bill Walsh created a path for many athletes, you can become the coach who creates a path for other coaches and athletes.

76

CHAPTER 10

MORE TOOLS IN THE TOOLBOX

As I was putting The ATHLETE Formula together, I realized there were some things I thought applied to The ATHLETE Formula but did not fit nicely into the seven-step process. I thought I would be doing coaches and athletes a disservice if I did not include them in the program somehow. So, here's a buffet of thoughts, ideas, concepts, and examples that I think will be helpful.

A Coach for the Coach

As a coach, you do not need to feel as though you have all the answers. Maybe you lack certain knowledge or your athlete is experiencing a problem that is beyond your expertise. In these situations, seek out coaching or mentoring yourself. Read a book or watch a YouTube video. Record what the athlete may be doing and watch it alone or with other trusted confidants; you might see what he is doing wrong. Baseball Hall of Famer Tony Gwynn was famous for watching videos of himself and how to improve his hitting. Seek guidance from others who have experience and have had success in the area you are trying to help your athlete improve upon. This may even include their competitors.

For example, NBA legend Kobe Bryant used to ask older players on other teams, like Michael Jordan and Gary Payton, about ways to improve their game. It may be intimidating to ask somebody else, even a competitor, for assistance. However, do not underestimate how some people love helping others. People may be honored (or feel validated) that another person holds them in high enough regard that their opinion is valued. Be aware. There will be some people who will turn you down for assistance. These people may not have time or are not good at mentoring. Other people may feel threatened or exhibit a type of narcissism where they claim they worked hard and succeeded on their own. These people may have worked hard, but NOBODY is completely self-sufficient. Regardless, this is a time to be resilient. Keep searching and seeking out people and other resources who are willing and able to help.

If you do not have access to a Hall of Famer to query (which you probably don't), all is not lost. The point is to find somebody who knows more about something than you, such as another coach or someone else with relevant experience. Maybe your neighbor played baseball in college; ask him for at least a few pointers on how to help your athlete. The goal is to look for resources outside of yourself to help your athlete become better than he is right now.

Learn to Pivot

As a coach, you might find that the expectations you had for a particular athlete are not in the cards. The dreams and aspirations you have for this athlete do not look like they will come true or provide that nice Hollywood ending you wanted. It is also possible that the dreams and aspirations are not coming true in a way that was planned or anticipated. That's fine. As I said before, a backup may not become a starter, but there are excellent opportunities for him to develop ways that help others on the team develop. The athlete may learn to develop his own set of coaching skills. There may be a log jam of athletes who want to play quarterback, but there are other positions with less competition, so have your athlete work on other skills like blocking and pass-catching to play tight end. If an athlete is playing soccer, he may want to play offense because that is who scores the goals; there is a lot of competition for those positions. Try encouraging the athlete to play defense. Make the primary goal to have the athlete contribute in ways that will increase his playing time.

Mariano Rivera, as discussed earlier, did not become a starting pitcher but developed his skills to become a great relief pitcher. NBA coach Rick Carlisle had an underwhelming NBA career, sitting on the bench for much of it. However, he parlayed his opportunity to become a successful assistant coach and has become an NBA champion head coach by embracing such a role early in his career. Not accomplishing your dream is not failure. Dreams are fantasies that can turn your reality into a nightmare. They are good starting points, but do not allow them to interfere with your athlete's opportunity to have productive experiences. Very rarely is an athlete going to be the very best where he is markedly better than his competition. Often, the fastest and best way to get more playing time is to be willing to take on roles that others do not wish to. Are there a lot of athletes on your team who want to be a starting pitcher or play shortstop? Encourage your athlete to be a relief pitcher or play in the outfield. Focusing on his willingness to do other things will result in more playing time and ways to contribute to the team's success.

CONCLUSION OF The ATHLETE Formula

The beauty of The ATHLETE Formula is that while it is geared toward athletics, the lessons apply to a lifetime of learning, growth, and development in any field. Ultimately, I **hope** that every leader (coach, manager, supervisor, professional, etc.) who uses this on his trainees will make each of them productive professionals. It is my aspiration that any leader who uses The ATHLETE Formula on his professionals will improve their performance to the point that they become stars in their given profession. However, The ATHLETE Formula is not a movie with a Hollywood ending where everything wraps up happily ever after. Again, sports is a microcosm of life, where even the best performers can lose more than they win.

The ATHLETE Formula is a guide to help humans manage inevitable failure and develop resiliency. It helps eliminate frustration and sets realistic bars for success and developing new skills. Are there outliers out there who were born with tremendous physical talent? Sure. Maybe there are a few who were born with physical gifts that most of us do not have. However, a person's mental makeup is often the difference between an athletic career that never progresses or one that keeps getting better. As much fun as sports can be, they are games that test our ability to deal with adversity. There is typically only one champion every year, and everyone else loses. Sports is a game where people need to learn how to bounce back after losing. Those who bounce back best tend to win more, but nobody has ever **not failed**. That is the essence of The ATHLETE Formula, where individuals learn how to rally back after losing. Success is ultimately a process, and The ATHLETE Formula is simply a process playbook. While coaching your athletes, you can take the attitude of Michael Jordan, who has said, "I have failed over and over again in my life…and that is why I succeed." Never underestimate the power you have over athletes for good. As the legendary football coach Ara Parseghian said, "A good coach will make his players see what they can be rather than what they are." Help someone see what they can be.

APPENDIX

QUICK GUIDE

This Quick Guide will help you with each of the seven steps of The ATHLETE Formula. Obviously, you will need to tailor these resources to your particular situation.

GOAL-SETTING 101: A common method of goal-setting is to have SMART goals.[16] SMART goals are:

- SPECIFIC: What is it that I want to accomplish with the athlete?

- MEASURABLE: In some activities, this might be harder to measure. However, how will you and the athlete know that a particular goal was accomplished?

- ACHIEVABLE: How can this goal be accomplished? You and the athlete may have to develop micro-goals when using shaping principles.

- RELEVANT: Does this goal seem relevant? Is the goal going to get you and the athlete to a place he wants to be?

---

16 Doran, G. T. (1981). "There's a S.M.A.R.T. Way to Write Management's Goals and Objectives" (PDF). Management Review, 70 (11): 35–36.

- TIME-BOUND: When can this goal (or micro-goal) be realistically accomplished? A time frame may be developed, but adjustments might need to be made.
  - (RECOMMENDATION: *Another type of goal that can be incorporated into the goal setting process is creating a realistic goal where the athlete will practice this skill set; for example, doing it three times per week for one hour.*)

COGNITIVE BEHAVIORAL THERAPY (CBT 101): CBT utilizes the accurate understanding of our thoughts to purposefully change reactions and behaviors. Our internal thoughts are viewed as mechanisms for change.

- Focusing on thoughts that produce feelings

- Goal-oriented

- Helps to understand a distorted belief system

COGNITIVE DISTORTIONS: These are types of flawed thinking. CBT is used to confront and combat these distortions. The goal is to help the athlete be more equipped to develop skills to properly process difficult situations.

- PERSONALIZATION: The attribution of the negative feelings of others and the world around them.
  - *(Example) A gymnastics coach is cross, so a gymnast automatically assumes that it is her fault.*

- EMOTIONAL REASONING: The distortion that occurs when feelings are considered as facts.
  - *(Example) Someone saying, "I feel that way, therefore, it must be true."*

- BLACK AND WHITE THINKING: A distortion that occurs when things are all or nothing.

    - *(Example) Someone might believe he has to be perfect or he is a failure.*

- OVERGENERALIZATION: Coming to broad, negative conclusions based on a single, insignificant event.

    - *(Example) I gave up a home run; therefore, I must not be a good pitcher.*

- CONTROL FALLACIES: A distortion in which a person feels that everything that happens is either ONLY a result of external actions or ONLY of their own behavior.

    - *(Example) Believing that your work is not good because you're dealing with disruptive coworkers.*

- CATASTROPHIZING: Distortion in which a person assumes or expects that the worst is going to happen.

    - *(Example) Believing that a small error at work is going to result in you being fired.*

GLOSSARY

ASPIRATION: A strong desire to achieve something high or great.

AUTHORITARIAN LEADERSHIP: Also known as coercive or dictatorial leadership, authoritarian leaders tend to keep all the decision-making authority for themselves when it comes to policies, procedures, tasks, structures, rewards, and punishment.

COGNITIVE DISTORTION: An exaggerated or irrational thought pattern involved in the onset or perpetuation of psychopathological states, such as depression and anxiety. Cognitive distortions are thoughts that cause individuals to perceive reality inaccurately.

CONFIDENCE: The belief in oneself and one's powers or abilities.

DEFENSE MECHANISM: Unconscious psychological processes employed to defend against feelings of anxiety and unacceptable impulses at the level of consciousness.

EMOTION: A conscious mental reaction (such as anger or fear) subjectively experienced as a strong feeling usually directed toward a specific object and typically accompanied by physiological and behavioral changes in the body.

LEGACY: Something transmitted by or received from an ancestor or predecessor or from the past.

MOOD: A conscious state of mind or predominant emotion.

SHAPING: The procedure that involves reinforcing behaviors that are closer to the target behavior, also known as successive approximations.

STRESS INOCULATION: Method intended to help individuals prepare themselves in advance to handle stressful events successfully and with a minimum of upset.

TACTICS: The art or skill of employing available means to accomplish an end; a system or mode of procedure.

THOUGHT: The act of thinking about or considering something, an idea or opinion, or a set of ideas about a particular subject.

TROUBLESHOOTING: Discovering why something does not work effectively and making suggestions about how to improve it.

BIOGRAPHY

I am a licensed clinical psychologist living in Virginia with my wife, two children, and a dog. I grew up in Illinois, near Chicago. For my entire life, I have been a sports fan. However, my life path led me toward psychology. I have worked in capacities where I have spent considerable time supporting law enforcement and the Department of Defense. I have also been in private practice for much of my career, and I am a behavioral health officer in the U.S. Army.

Throughout my experience working with various populations, I have often been excited by the idea of dealing with failure and improving performance. As a sports fan and a behavioral expert, I saw how those ideas aligned nicely with the profession of sports. When I helped my son R.J. improve in soccer, I knew I had something. I have realized that sports is really a microcosm of all human behavior related to coping with failure and bouncing back after setbacks. Sports takes place in a more structured environment where lots of relevant statistics are readily available. Real life is not as confined, but many of the same principles are present. In the end, I have come to learn that humans are more alike than they are different. The ATHLETE Formula program is made up of the various aspects of cognitive behavioral therapy and learning theory that are combined to be used on baseball diamonds, soccer fields, and in schools but can just as easily be used in boardrooms.